🎉 **Hey There, Awesome Reader!**
Welcome to
"The BEST of Books"

Where every page brings out the BEST in YOU!

✨ Imagination? Check!
💖 Kindness? You bet!
🦄 Adventures, giggles, and feel-good fun? All inside!

This series includes six illustrated storybooks and one super fun coloring book, all created to help YOU shine bright, dream big, and be your amazing self. Whether you're reading a story or coloring your own, there's no wrong way to play.
Your way is the BEST way!
So, grab your favorite book, flip the page,
and let your BEST shine through!

🌟 Explore the full series at:

(www.TheBESTOfBooks.com)

All Books In The BEST of Series. . . by J. R. Philp

- **The BEST of America**
- **The BEST of Christmas**
- **The BEST of Life Vol. 1**
- **The BEST of All of Us Vol. 2**
- **The BEST of Fun Vol. 3**
- **The BEST of Colors and Shapes Vol. 4**
- **My Coloring Book is The BEST**

Copyright © 2018 by J. R. Philp
All rights reserved.

No part of this publication may be reproduced, stored in a retrieval system, or transmitted in any form or by any means - electronic, mechanical, photocopying, recording, or otherwise - without the prior written permission of the publisher, except in the case of brief quotations used in reviews or articles.

For information regarding bulk purchases, educational use, or special editions, please contact the publisher at: info@seibroinc.com

This book is a work of original authorship.
Story by J R Philp | Illustrated by Chris Padovano
Layout, design, and typography by Seibro Inc
Published by Seibro Inc
Tampa, FL

Printed in the United States of America
First Edition, 2018

TheBestofBooks.com

10 9 8 7 6 5 4 3 2 1

"America is the Best and the greatest country in the world.

We are a nation of many backgrounds, nationalities, and we have a common bond of freedom.

This book is dedicated to the special pride we have when we wave our flag, sing our national anthem, salute our service men and women, and cheer our Air Force flyovers.

God Bless America!"

Allegiance

The BEST promise in the world... our Pledge to our Flag!

"I pledge allegiance to the Flag of the United States of America, and to the Republic for which it stands, one Nation under God, indivisible, with liberty and justice for all."

The Star-Spangled Banner

O say can you see, by the dawn's early light,
What so proudly we hailed at the twilight's last gleaming,
Whose broad stripes and bright stars through the perilous fight,
O'er the ramparts we watched, were so gallantly streaming?
And the rockets' red glare, the bombs bursting in air,
Gave proof through the night that our flag was still there;
O say does that star-spangled banner yet wave
O'er the land of the free and the home of the brave?

Francis Scott Key

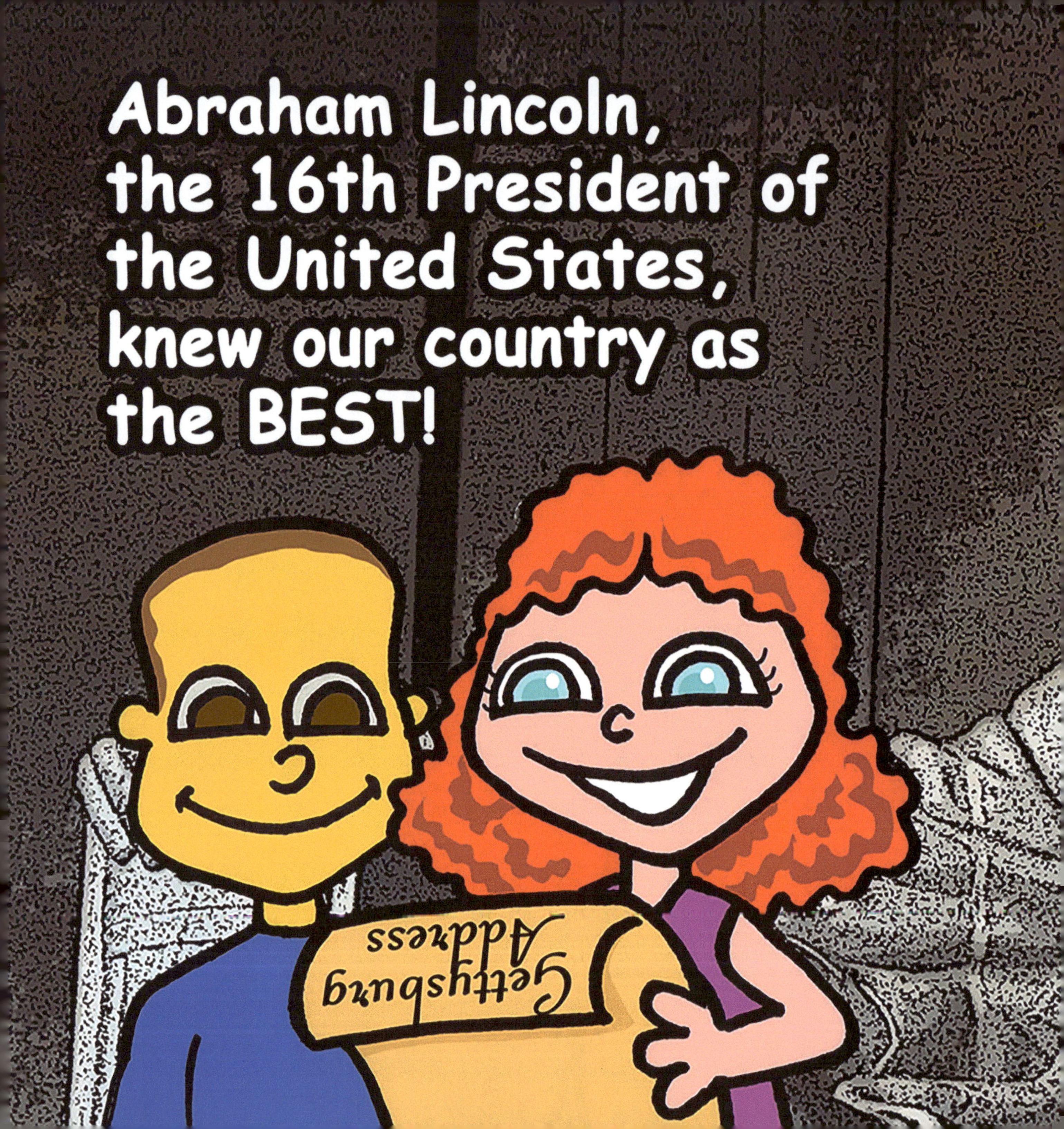

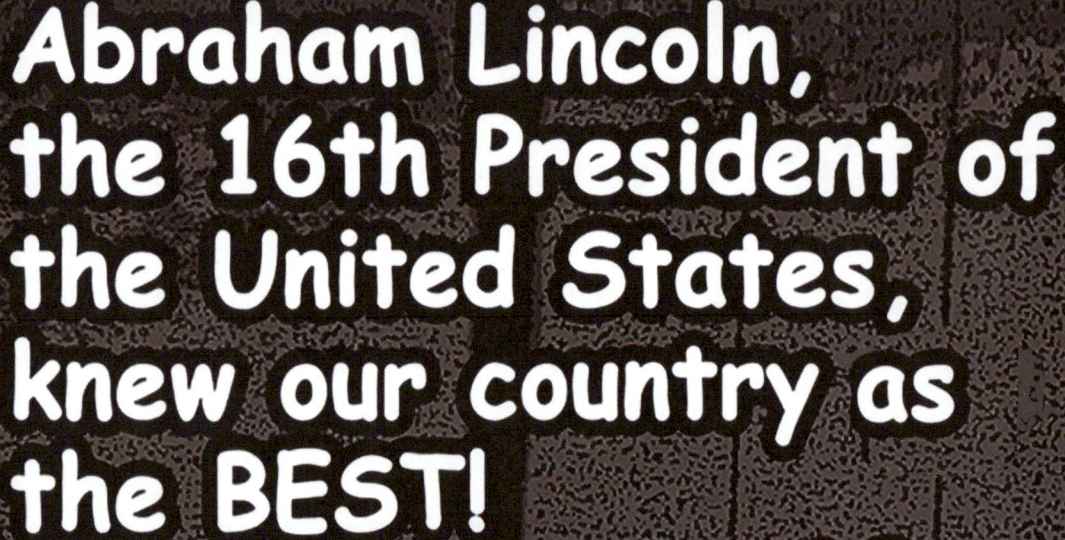

Abraham Lincoln, the 16th President of the United States, knew our country as the BEST!
Gettysburg Address

🎈 About The BEST of Books Series

Get ready to dream big, think kind thoughts, and smile from the inside out!
Each book in "The BEST of Books" series celebrates the little things that make life magical, like a giggle, a good idea, or a splash of color. Whether you're reading with a friend or coloring on your own, these stories remind us that the BEST moments are often the simplest ones.

✨ Collect them all and share the joy:

- ❖ "The BEST of Christmas"
- ❖ "The BEST of America"
- ❖ "The BEST of Life"
- ❖ "The BEST of All of Us"
- ❖ "The BEST of Colors and Shapes"
- ❖ "The BEST of Fun"
- ❖ "My Coloring Book Is The BEST"

📚 Keep exploring at:
www.TheBESTOfBooks.com

www.ingramcontent.com/pod-product-compliance
Lightning Source LLC
Chambersburg PA
CBHW041529070526
44586CB00002B/25